The Dominie Collection of

Aes
Fak

The Hare
and the Tortoise

Retold by Alan Trussell-Cullen

Illustrated by Edward Mooney

Dominie Press, Inc.

The hare was always boasting.

"I am the fastest runner in the whole forest!" he said. "I can run faster than anyone else! In fact, I am the fastest runner in the whole world!"

The other animals were tired of listening to the hare telling them how fast he was. They tried to ignore him, but this didn't stop his boasting.

One day the hare said he had a wonderful idea. "Why don'l we have a race to see who is the fastest animal in the world? We could run through the forest to the giant oak tree and finish back here in the farmer's field!"

But none of the other animals wanted to race against the hare.

"That proves it, then!" said the hare. "I must be the fastest runner in the world!"

Just then, a tortoise came slowly plodding along.
"I'll race you," said the tortoise.

The hare began to laugh. "You'll race me?" he
said, holding his sides. "You? A slow old tortoise?"

"Of course," said the tortoise.

The next day, the fox was chosen to start the race. "On your marks!" he said. "Get set! Go!"

The hare immediately sprinted off across the field and into the forest.

The tortoise started off, too, but much more slowly.

The hare was having a great time. As he bounded through the forest, he sang to himself:

"I am the fastest! I am the greatest!"

Soon the hare was far ahead of the tortoise. He reached the giant oak tree. Then he turned and began to run back through the forest again.

On his way back, he met the tortoise.

"You might as well give up now," said the hare. "I'm nearly finished already!"

But the tortoise just kept plodding on and on through the forest. "I must keep going! I must keep going!" he said.

Soon the hare came to the edge of the forest. He could see the farmer's field and the animals waiting at the finish line.

But it was a hot, sunny day.

"This is such an easy race!" he said to himself. "I've even got time for a little nap."

He found a patch of nice, soft grass and decided to curl up for a snooze in the sun.

Meanwhile the tortoise kept plodding on and on. "I must keep going! I must keep going!" he said. He reached the giant oak tree. Then he turned around and started back through the forest.

"I must keep going! I must keep going!" said the tortoise.

When the tortoise came out of the forest, he saw the hare sleeping in the sun. But he just kept plodding on and on.

"I must keep going! I must keep going!" he said.

Soon the animals saw the tortoise approaching the finish line. They were amazed. They began to cheer.

"Come on, tortoise! You can do it!" they shouted.

The tortoise said, "I must keep going! I must keep going!"

The loud cheering and shouting woke up the hare. When he opened his eyes, he saw that the tortoise was very close to the finish line.

"Oh no!" shouted the hare. And he began to run! He began to sprint! He ran as fast as he could!

But he was too late. The tortoise crossed the finish line ahead of him.

The hare was so ashamed, he just crept away.

"Well done, tortoise!" shouted the animals. "But what was the secret of your success?"

"It's simple really," said the tortoise. "Slow and steady wins the race."